MATTHEW
FOR BEGINNERS

MIKE MAZZALONGO

STUDENT WORKBOOK

BibleTalk.TV

DOWNLOAD OUR APP

Copyright 2022 BibleTalk.tv

All our material is licensed under the Creative Commons Attribution-NonCommercial-ShareAlike License.
This means you can use it almost however you need.
The only thing you can't do is re-sell it.

Download it.   Print it.   Teach it.   Share it.

Table of Contents

1. Introduction to Matthew's Gospel — 6
2. The New Testament Canon — 10
3. Beginnings of the Gospel: Narrative #1 — 16
4. Sermon on the Mount: Discourse #1 — 22
5. Jesus' Power: Narrative #2 — 28
6. Names and Mission of the Apostles: Discourse #2 — 32
7. Jesus Faces Skepticism: Narrative #3 — 36
8. The Use of Parables in Jesus' Teaching: Discourse #3 — 40
9. Ministry to the Masses, Ministry to the Few: Narrative #4 — 44
10. Relationships in the Kingdom: Discourse #4 — 48
11. Marriage – Divorce – Remarriage: Narrative #5 — 52
12. Rejection and Judgement: Discourse #5 — 58
13. From Passover to Communion: Narrative #6 — 62

Matthew for Beginners

Mike Mazzalongo

This series provides an in-depth look at the most well-structured gospel record originally designed to address Jewish questions about Jesus but later used by the early church as a primer for new Christians.

bibletalk.tv/matthew

1. Introduction to Matthew's Gospel

This introductory lesson will review the historical, political and social conditions that led up to and include the times in which this gospel record was written.

Intro _____

Historical Background

Persian – 536-336 BC

- 586 BC _____
- 539 BC _____
- 520 BC _____

Intertestamentary Period – 400 yrs.

- Historical Books _____

- Commentaries _____

- Apocrypha _____

- Pseudipigrapha _____

Greek Period – 333-167 BC _____

320-198 BC – Egypt _____
_____
_____

198-167 – Syria _____
_____
_____

Maccabean Period – 167-63 BC _____
_____
_____

- Pharisees _____
  _____

- Sadducees _____
  _____

- Essenes _____
  _____

- Zealots _____
  _____

- Herodians _____
  _____

Roman Period – 63 BC – New Testament _____
_____
_____
_____

  Herod _____
  _____
  _____

Pontius Pilate _____
_____
_____

Calendar Change – BC / AD

_____
_____
_____

- Year #1-Rome -------------- Year #753 – Christ ------------- Year #1279 - New Calendar Proposed
- New Year #1- Christ ------------- Year #526- Calendar Changed
- Corrected Year - #749
- Christ Born - 4 BC.

Roman empire helped evangelize:
1. Tax Romana _____
2. Roman Roads _____
3. Greek Language _____
_____
_____
_____

Palestine in New Testament Times

_____
_____

Social Background _____
_____
_____

Class Division:

- Aristocracy _____

- Pharisees _____

- Common People _____

- Publicans _____

- Sinners _____

- Scaves _____

Social Problems

_____
_____
_____
_____

Religious Life

_____
_____
_____
_____

Into this world comes Jesus Christ

_____
_____
_____
_____

Assignment

1. Read Matthew Chapters 1-3
2. Write down:
    - Main section titles
    - Something new you have learned.

2. The New Testament Canon

In this lesson we continue to examine background information about Matthew himself and a closer look at the purpose and structure of his book.

Intro - Review of Lesson #1

_____
_____

Authorship of Matthew

_____
_____

New Testament Canon

_____
_____

Acts 2:14-21 _____
_____
_____

II Timothy 3:15 _____
_____
_____

Matthew 28:20 _____
_____
_____

John 14:26 _____
_____
_____

I Corinthians 2:6-13 _____
_____
_____

Revelation 1:1-2 _____
_____
_____

II Peter 1:15-21 _____
_____
_____

II Peter 3:14-16 _____
_____
_____

Events that led to the collection and formation of the New Testament Canon:
- The Apostles _____
  _____
  _____

- Heresies within the church _____
  _____
  _____

- Oppression by the _____
  _____
  _____

Criteria for inclusion in the church.

1. Written _____
   _____
   _____

2. Well circulated _____
   _____
   _____

3. Accepted by church in the _____ age.
   _____
   _____

New Testament Canon

_____
_____

Matthew and his writings.
_____
_____

Purpose and structure of Matthew.

A. Defense _____
   _____
   _____

B. Manual _____
   _____
   _____

Structure of Matthew

Six Narrative _____

_____
_____
_____
_____
_____
_____

Five Discourse _____

_____
_____
_____
_____
_____
_____

Assignments

- List narrative bullet points in Narrative #1 on worksheet.
- Begin reading Discourse #1.

IV. NARRATIVE 13:53 - 17:27	IV. DISCOURSE 18:1-35	V. NARRATIVE 19:1 - 22:46
Jesus' Identity	Relationships	Ministry in Judea

V. DISCOURSE 23:1 - 25:46	VI. NARRATIVE 26:1 - 28:20
Rejection and Judgment	Death/Resurrection/Commission

I. NARRATIVE 1:1 - 4:23	I. DISCOURSE 5:1 - 7:29	II. NARRATIVE 8:1 - 9:34
Beginnings of the Gospel	Sermon on the Mount	Jesus' Power

II. DISCOURSE 9:35 - 10:42	III. NARRATIVE 11:1 - 12:50	III. DISCOURSE 13:1-52
Discourse to the Twelve	Jesus and Skepticism	Parables of the Kingdom

3. Beginnings of the Gospel: Narrative #1

This lesson begins the comments and explanations of the material that Matthew lists in his opening narrative which include Jesus' genealogy, birth, escape to Egypt and return to Nazareth. (Matthew 1:1-4:23)

_____
_____

Intro - Review

- Gospel written by _____ in _____ AD.
- Written as a _____ of the faith.
- Written mostly for _____ readers.
- Organized into _____ narratives and 5 _____.
- Also used as _____ for _____ Christians.

Narrative #1

Genealogy – Matthew 1:1-17 _____
_____
_____

Genealogy given to _____
_____
_____
_____

Differences between Matthew and Luke's genealogy:

- ○ _____
  _____
  _____
  _____

- ○ _____
  _____
  _____
  _____

- o _____
  _____
  _____
- o _____
  _____
  _____

Women in Matthew's Genealogy
- o _____Tamar_____
- o _____
- o _____
- o _____
- o _____Mary_____

Birth of Jesus – Matthew 1:18-25 _____
_____
_____
_____

Wise Men – Matthew 2:1-15
_____
_____

Magi were priests, counselors, astrologers to the king in Persia. _____
_____
_____

Escape to Egypt and Return – Matthew 2:13-23
_____
_____

Fulfillment of Hosea 11:1 prophecy. _____
_____
_____

John the Baptist – Matthew 3:1-17
_____
_____
_____
_____

Greek words for Baptism:
- Rhantizo _____
- Ballo _____
- Baptioz _____

_____
_____
_____

Temptations – Matthew 4:1-11
Three temptations are recorded:

1. Cast Doubt _____
_____
_____

2. Use the Word to _____
_____
_____

3. Satan appeals to Jesus' human nature _____
_____
_____

Galilee and the Disciples – Matthew 4:12-25

_____
_____
_____
_____
_____
_____
_____

Assignments

- Read Discourse #1 – Matthew 5:1 - 7:29
- List subject headings on worksheet
- Keep a record of your "nuggets"

IV. NARRATIVE 13:53 - 17:27	Jesus' Identity	
IV. DISCOURSE 18:1-35	Relationships	
V. NARRATIVE 19:1 - 22:46	Ministry in Judea	
V. DISCOURSE 23:1 - 25:46	Rejection and Judgment	
VI. NARRATIVE 26:1 - 28:20	Death/Resurrection/Commission	

I. NARRATIVE 1:1 - 4:23	I. DISCOURSE 5:1 - 7:29	II. NARRATIVE 8:1 - 9:34
Beginnings of the Gospel 1. Genealogy- 1:1-17 2. Birth- 1:18-25 3. Magi- 2:1-12 4. Egypt & Return- 2:13-23 5. John the Baptist- 3:1-17 6. Temptations- 4:1-11 7. Galilee & Disciples- 4:12-25	Sermon on the Mount	Jesus' Power
II. DISCOURSE 9:35 - 10:42	III. NARRATIVE 11:1 - 12:50	III. DISCOURSE 13:1-52
Discourse to the Twelve	Jesus and Skepticism	Parables of the Kingdom

4. Sermon on the Mount: Discourse #1

In this lesson we review the five main topics discussed by Jesus in His Sermon on the Mount. (Matthew 5:1-7:29)

_____
_____

Intro - Study Approach for Matthew

1. _____
2. _____
3. _____

Sermon on the Mount – Matthew 5:1 – 7:29

_____
_____

Sermon deals with five major topics:

a. _____ 5:1-16
b. _____ 5:17-48
c. _____ 6:1-34
d. _____ 7:1-12
e. _____ 7:13-29

_____
_____

Beatitudes – 5:3-16

Beatitudo - _____ - _____

_____
_____

Style used by rabbis who usually introduced a lesson with a question.

_____
_____

Disciples in the Kingdom are distinctive.

_____
_____

The Law – 5:17-48

Vs. 20 _____
_____
_____
_____

Compares those who _____ the law to the one who _____ the law.

_____
_____
_____
_____

Five areas of the law are discussed:

1. Murder – vs. 21 _____
_____
_____

2. Adultery – vs. 27 _____
_____
_____

3. Vows – vs. 33 _____
_____
_____

4. Justice – vs. 38 _____

_____

_____

5. Nationalism – vs. 43 _____

_____

_____

Relationship with God – 6:1-34

A proper relationship with God includes:

1. Practice _____

   _____

   _____

   _____

2. Prayer _____

   _____

   _____

   _____

3. Trust _____

   _____

   _____

   _____

Relationship with others - 7:1-12

Vs. 12 _____

_____

_____

_____

The way of life – 7:13-29

How to enter into life:

A. Enter by _____

B. Beware of _____

C. Don't just _____

Assignment

Read Narrative #2 – 8:1-9:34

I. NARRATIVE 1:1 - 4:23	I. DISCOURSE 5:1 - 7:29	II. NARRATIVE 8:1 - 9:34
Beginnings of the Gospel 1. Genealogy- 1:1-17 2. Birth- 1:18-25 3. Magi- 2:1-12 4. Egypt & Return 2:13-23 5. John the Baptist- 3:1-17 6. Temptations- 4:1-11 7. Galilee & Disciples- 4:12-25	Sermon on the Mount 1. Beatitudes- 5:1-16 2. The Law- 5:17-48 3. Relationship with God- 6:1-34 4. Relationship with others- 7:1-12 5. The way of life- 7:13-29	Jesus' Power

II. DISCOURSE 9:35 - 10:42	III. NARRATIVE 11:1 - 12:50	III. DISCOURSE 13:1-52
Discourse to the Twelve	Jesus and Skepticism	Parables of the Kingdom

5. Jesus' Power: Narrative #2

In this section Matthew describes 3 amazing days in Jesus' busy life. (Matthew 8:1-9:38)

_____

_____

Intro - Review

_____

_____

Three Days in the Life of Christ

John 21:25 _____

_____

Day #1

- _____
- _____
- _____
- _____
- _____

Day #2

- _____
- _____
- _____
- _____

Day #3

- _____
- _____
- _____
- _____

- Nature of Kingdom _____
- Power of Kingdom _____
- Way to Kingdom _____
- Entrance to Kingdom _____

Most important theme is _____.

Narrative #2 – 8:1-9:38

Miracles:

1. _____
2. _____
3. _____

Teaching – 8:18-22

1. _____
2. _____

Miracles – 9:18-34

1. _____
2. _____
3. _____
4. _____
5. _____

Teaching – 9:9-17

1. _____
2. _____
3. _____

The Patch and Wineskin

_____
_____

Miracles – 9:18-34

1. _____
2. _____
3. _____

Summary – 9:35-38

_____
_____
_____
_____

Assignment

Read Discourse #2 – Matthew 9:35-10:42

I. NARRATIVE 1:1-4:23	I. DISCOURSE 5:1-7:29	II. NARRATIVE 8:1-9:34

Beginnings of the Gospel
 	
I. Genealogy — 1:1-17
II. Birth — 1:18-25
III. Magi — 2:1-12
IV. Egypt — 2:13-15
V. Massacre & Return — 2:16-23
VI. John the Baptist — 3:1-17
VII. Temptations — 4:1-11
VIII. Galilee & Disciples — 4:12-25
	Sermon on the Mount
	
	I. Beatitudes 5:1-16
	II. The Law 5:17-48
	III. Relationship with God 6:1-34
	IV. Relationship with others 7:1-12
	V. The way of life 7:13-29
		Jesus' Power
		
		I. Miracles — 8:1-17
		  A. Leper Cleansed
		  B. Centurion's slave
		  C. Peter's mother-in-law
		II. Teaching - would be disciples 8:18-22
		III. Miracles — 8:23-9:8
		  A. Calming the storm
		  B. Cast out demons/Paralytic cured
		IV. Teaching — 9:9-17
		  A. Matthew called
		  B. Accusations
		  C. John's Disciples
		V. Miracles — 9:18-34
		  A. Official's daughter
		  B. Woman with hemorrhage
		  C. Dumb and demon possessed
		VI. Jesus, Lord of Harvest — 9:35-38

II. DISCOURSE 9:35-10:42 Discourse to the Twelve	III. NARRATIVE 11:1-12:50 Jesus and Skepticism	III. DISCOURSE 13:1-52 Parables of the Kingdom

6. Names and Mission of the Apostles: Discourse #2

Matthew lists the names of those chosen by Jesus to be His special messengers, and reviews the instructions and warnings Jesus gives them before sending them out on their first solo mission. (Matthew 10:1-42)

_____
_____

Intro - Review

_____
_____

Granting of Power – 10:1

_____
_____

Names and Mission of the Apostles – 10:2-4

_____
_____

They were:

1. Eyewitnesses _____
_____

2. They established _____
_____

3. They taught and recorded _____
_____

14 Apostles in all: _____
_____
_____
_____
_____

Instructions Concerning Their Mission – Mt. 10:5-42

Ministry to Israel – 10:5-15

A. Go to _____

B. Preach _____

C. Power to _____

D. What to _____

E. Method of _____

Warnings – 10:16-23

A. People will _____

B. Jesus will _____

C. Results _____

Instructions – 10:24-33

Don't _____

Don't _____

33

Failure _____

_____

Death _____

_____

Error _____

_____

Comment – 10:34-39

Gospel brings _____

_____

_____

Gospel demands _____

_____

_____

_____

Promise – 10:40-42

_____

_____

_____

Assignment

Read Narrative – Matthew 11:1-12:50

I. NARRATIVE 1:1-4:23 Beginnings of the Gospel	I. DISCOURSE 5:1-7:29 Sermon on the Mount	II. NARRATIVE 8:1-9:34 Jesus' Power

I. Genealogy — 1:1-17
II. Birth — 1:18-25
III. Magi — 2:1-12
IV. Egypt — 2:13-15
V. Massacre & Return — 2:16-23
VI. John the Baptist — 3:1-17
VII. Temptations — 4:1-11
VIII. Galilee & Disciples — 4:12-25
	I. Beatitudes 5:1-16
	II. The Law 5:17-48
	III. Relationship with God 6:1-34
	IV. Relationship with others 7:1-12
	V. The way of life 7:13-29
		I. Miracles — 8:1-17
		  A. Leper Cleansed
		  B. Centurion's slave
		  C. Peter's mother-in-law
		II. Teaching - would be disciples 8:18-22
		III. Miracles — 8:23-9:8
		  A. Calming the storm
		  B. Cast out demons/Paralytic cured
		IV. Teaching — 9:9-17
		  A. Matthew called
		  B. Accusations
		  C. John's Disciples
		V. Miracles — 9:18-34
		  A. Official's daughter
		  B. Woman with hemorrhage
		  C. Dumb and demon possessed
		VI. Jesus, Lord of Harvest — 9:35-38

II. DISCOURSE 9:35-10:42 Discourse to the Twelve	III. NARRATIVE 11:1-12:50 Jesus and Skepticism	III. DISCOURSE 13:1-52 Parables of the Kingdom

I. Granting of the power 10:1
II. Name of the Apostles 10:2-4
III. Instructions concerning their Mission
  A. Ministry to Israel 10:5-15
  B. Warning to people 10:16-23
  C. Instructions to Apostles 10:23-33
  D. Negative response to the gospel 10:34-39
  E. Promise to those who respond positively 10:40-42		

7. Jesus Faces Skepticism: Narrative #3

Matthew describes the aggressive questioning Jesus would begin to draw from the Jewish religious leaders as His ministry progressed. (Matthew 11:1-12:50)

_____
_____

Intro - Jesus' ministry begins powerfully:

- _____
- _____
- _____
- _____

Witness concerning John the Baptist – 11:2-30

Response to John – vs. 2-6

_____
_____

Witness concerning John – vs. 7-19

A. He was _____
_____
_____

B. He was _____
_____
_____

C. He had _____
_____
_____

D. He is not _____
_____
_____

E. He was _____
_____
_____

Reproach of cities that rejected John and Jesus – vs. 20-24

_____
_____
_____

Invitation and Promise – vs. 25-30

Jesus' Prayer:

   1. Gratitude _____
_____
_____

   2. Promise _____
_____
_____

   3. Invitation _____
_____
_____

Conflict with the Pharisees – 12:1-45

Accusation of Sabbath Breaking – vs. 1-14

_____
_____

    Harvesting the corn – vs. 1-8 _____
_____
_____

    Healing – vs. 9-14 _____
_____
_____

Fulfillment of Prophecy – vs. 15-21 _____

_____

Accusations of Association with Satan – vs. 22-23 _____

_____

_____

Jesus's Response – vs. 24-37:

- Illogical _____

_____

- Godly Power _____

_____

- Rebuke_____

_____

_____

Seeking a Sign – vs. 38-45

- Nineveh _____

_____

- Queen of Sheba _____

_____

- Man possessed with demon _____

_____

_____

Conflict with Family – vs. 46-50

_____

_____

_____

Assignment

Read Matthew 13:1-52

I. NARRATIVE 1:1-4:23	I. DISCOURSE 5:1-7:29	II. NARRATIVE 8:1-9:34
Beginnings of the Gospel	**Sermon on the Mount**	**Jesus' Power**

I. Genealogy — 1:1-17
II. Birth — 1:18-25
III. Magi — 2:1-12
IV. Egypt — 2:13-15
V. Massacre & Return — 2:16-23
VI. John the Baptist — 3:1-17
VII. Temptations — 4:1-11
VIII. Galilee & Disciples — 4:12-25
	I. Beatitudes 5:1-16
	II. The Law 5:17-48
	III. Relationship with God 6:1-34
	IV. Relationship with others 7:1-12
	V. The way of life 7:13-29
		I. Miracles · 8:1-17
		  A. Leper Cleansed
		  B. Centurion's slave
		  C. Peter's mother-in-law
		II. Teaching - would be disciples 8:18-22
		III. Miracles — 8:23-9:8
		  A. Calming the storm
		  B. Cast out demons/Paralytic cured
		IV. Teaching 9:9-17
		  A. Matthew called
		  B. Accusations
		  C. John's Disciples
		V. Miracles — 9:18-34
		  A. Official's daughter
		  B. Woman with hemorrhage
		  C. Dumb and demon possessed
		VI. Jesus, Lord of Harvest — 9:35-38

II. DISCOURSE 9:35-10:42	III. NARRATIVE 11:1-12:50	III. DISCOURSE 13:1-52
Discourse to the Twelve	**Jesus and Skepticism**	**Parables of the Kingdom**

I. Granting of the power 10:1
II. Name of the Apostles 10:2-4
III. Instructions concerning their Mission
  A. Ministry to Israel 10:5-15
  B. Warning to people 10:16-23
  C. Instructions to Apostles 10:23-33
  D. Negative response to the gospel 10:34-39
  E. Promise to those who respond positively 10:40-42
	I. Witness concerning John 11:1-30
	  A. Response to John's question
	  B. Witness concerning question
	  C. Reproach on cities
	  D. Invitation to those who accept John
	II. Conflict with Pharisees 12:1-45
	  A. Accusations of Sabbath Breaking
	  B. Accusations of association
	  C. Seeking a sign
	III. Conflict with Jesus' Family 12:46-50	

8. The Use of Parables in Jesus' Teaching: Discourse #3

This lesson will examine the reasons why Jesus used parables in His teaching ministry and what rules we need to follow in order to understand their original meaning and how to draw applications from them today.
(Matthew 13:1-52)

_____
_____

Intro - Jesus used parables in His teaching for two main reasons:

   1. _____
_____
   2. _____
_____

Parables

_____
_____

Good teaching method:

      1. _____
      2. _____

Parables were usually an imaginary story used to illustrate _____
_____
_____
_____

Jesus did not _____
_____
_____
_____

Basic rules of interpretation:

A. Look for the _____

_____

_____

B. Avoid _____

_____

_____

C. Parables illustrate truth _____

_____

_____

D. Look for the meaning _____

_____

_____

E. Jesus and His _____

_____

_____

Kingdom Parables

Matthew has _____ parables + one _____

_____

_____

_____

Kingdom parables: Three Views

1. The Kingdom is coming _____

_____

_____

2. The Kingdom is fully _____
_____
_____

3. The Kingdom has been _____
_____
_____

Parables in Matthew

_____
_____
_____

13:1-9 _____
_____
_____
_____

13:10-17 _____
_____
_____
_____

13:18-23 _____
_____
_____
_____
_____

Remaining Kingdom parables in Matthew 13:

Parables   _____ vs. 24-30
            _____ vs. 31-32
            _____ vs. 33

            Parenthetical statement   vs. 34-35
            Explanation of Wheat and Tares vs. 36-43

Parables   _____ vs. 44
            _____ vs. 45-46
            _____ vs. 47-50
            Summary Statement   vs. 51-52

Assignment

Pick two _____

Answer
1. _____
2. _____
3. _____

9. Ministry to the Masses, Ministry to the Few: Narrative #4

Jesus performs miracles for the crowds as well as private demonstrations of His power for His Apostles in order to strengthen their faith and prepare them for His own suffering and death on the cross. (Matthew 13:53-17:27)

_____
_____

Intro - Chapter 13-17 – Ministry in Galilee

_____
_____

Last of great miracles.
- Feeding _____
- Healing _____
- Transfiguration _____
- Mouth of _____
- Healing of _____

Final ministry in Jerusalem will include
- Teaching _____
- Triumphal _____
- Judgment _____
- Suffering _____

Rejection – Matthew 13:53-14:12

_____
_____
_____
_____
_____

44

Ministry to the Masses

1. Feeding 5,000 – Matthew 14:13-21

2. Healing – Matthew 14:34-36

3. Healing a Gentile – Matthew 15:21-28

4. Healing – Matthew 15:29-31

5. Feeing 4,000 – Matthew 15:32-39

6. Healing boy – Matthew 17:9-13

Response to Accusers

Transgressing tradition – 15:1-20

Ask for a sign – 16:1-12

Ministry to the Apostles

Miracles:

A. Walking on water – Matthew 14:22-33

B. Transfiguration – Matthew 17:1-8

C. Coin in the fish – Matthew 17:24-27

D. Teaching

    1. What defiles – Matthew 15:15-20

2. Warning about Pharisees – Matthew 16:1-12

3. Response to Peter's confession – Matthew 16:13-19

   – Jesus teaches them beyond this confession of faith.

   – The "Keys" of the Kingdom is the ability to open the doors to the Kingdom in heaven.

4. Prophecy concerning the crucifixion.
   – Mt. 16:21-28
   – Mt. 17:9-13
   – Mt. 17:22-23

Lessons from the prophecy:

A. Resurrection – Matthew 16:21

B. Discipleship – Matthew 16:24-26

C. Prophets – Matthew 17:10

Assignment

Read Discourse #4 – Matthew 18:1-35

10. Relationships in the Kingdom: Discourse #4

In this passage Jesus will explain the nature of relationships that people have in the Kingdom and how to repair them when they are broken.
(Matthew 18:1-35)

_____
_____

Intro - Jesus' teaching about the Kingdom in Matthew:

1. Kingdom _____ 4:17
2. Kinds _____ 5:3-20
3. Who _____ 6:13
4. The Importance _____ 6:33
5. Who _____ 7:21
6. How _____ 11:11
7. Not _____ 13:1-23
8. God _____ 13:24-30; 47-50
9. Kingdom _____ 13:31-33
10. Kingdom _____ 13:44-46

Relationships within the Kingdom

Character of people in the Kingdom

Vs. 1-5 _____
_____

Warning against offenses

Vs. 6-10 _____
_____

Parable – vs. 11-14 _____
_____

Dealing with conflict _____
_____

Vs. 15-17 _____

_____

_____

Authority _____

Vs. 18-20 _____

Maintaining Relationships

_____

_____

    A. The Old Standard – vs. 21-22 _____

    B. New Standard _____

    C. Authority _____

Lessons

When it comes to offenses:

A. Don't _____

B. Deal _____

C. Forgive _____

IV. NARRATIVE 13:53-17:27	IV. DISCOURSE 18:1-35	V. NARRATIVE 19:1-22:46

Jesus' Identity
 	
I. Rejection at Nazareth - 13:53-14:12
II. Ministry to the Masses
  A. 5,000 fed - 14:13-21
  B. Healings by touching - 14:34-36
  C. Woman's daughter healed - 15:21-28
  D. Healings of sick and crippled - 15:20-31
  E. 4,000 fed - 15:32-39
  F. Healing of epileptic boy - 17:9-13
III. Response to Pharisees
  A. Breaking traditions - 15:1-20
  B. Ask for a sign - 16:1-12
IV. Ministry to Apostles
  A. By miracles performed
    1. Walking on water - 14:22-33
    2. Transfiguration - 17:1-8
    3. Coin in the fish - 17:9-17
  B. By teaching concerning
    1. True defilement - 15:15-20
    2. Teaching of the Pharisees - 16:1-12
    3. The church - 16:13-20
    4. The crucifixion - 16:21-28, 17:9-13, 17:22-33
	Relationships
	
	I. Basic Premise: Care for Each Soul 18:1-5
	  A. Character of people in Kingdom
	  B. Warning about offenses - 18:6-10
	  Parable about lost sheep - 18:11-14
	II. Dealing with Conflict: Direct Confrontation - 18:15-20
	  A. Procedure - 18:15-17
	  B. Authority - 18:18-20
	III. Basis for Relationships: Unconditional Forgiveness
	  A. The old standard - 18:21
	  B. Standard in the Kingdom - 18:22
	  Parable - 18:23-34
	  C. Summary - 18:35
		Ministry in Judea

V. DISCOURSE 23:1-25:46	VI. NARRATIVE 26:1-28:20
Rejection and Judgment	Death/Resurrection/Commission

I. NARRATIVE 1:1-4:23	I. DISCOURSE 5:1-7:29	II. NARRATIVE 8:1-9:34
Beginnings of the Gospel	**Sermon on the Mount**	**Jesus' Power**

I. Genealogy — 1:1-17
II. Birth — 1:18-25
III. Magi — 2:1-12
IV. Egypt — 2:13-15
V. Massacre & Return — 2:16-23
VI. John the Baptist — 3:1-17
VII. Temptations — 4:1-11
VIII. Galilee & Disciples — 4:12-25
	I. Beatitudes 5:1-16
	II. The Law 5:17-48
	III. Relationship with God 6:1-34
	IV. Relationship with others 7:1-12
	V. The way of life 7:13-29
		I. Miracles — 8:1-17
		  A. Leper Cleansed
		  B. Centurion's slave
		  C. Peter's mother-in-law
		II. Teaching - would be disciples 8:18-22
		III. Miracles — 8:23-9:8
		  A. Calming the storm
		  B. Cast out demons/Paralytic cured
		IV. Teaching 9:9-17
		  A. Matthew called
		  B. Accusations
		  C. John's Disciples
		V. Miracles — 9:18-34
		  A. Official's daughter
		  B. Woman with hemorrhage
		  C. Dumb and demon possessed
		VI. Jesus, Lord of Harvest — 9:35-38

II. DISCOURSE 9:35-10:42	III. NARRATIVE 11:1-12:50	III. DISCOURSE 13:1-52
Discourse to the Twelve	**Jesus and Skepticism**	**Parables of the Kingdom**

I. Granting of the power 10:1
II. Name of the Apostles 10:2-4
III. Instructions concerning their Mission
  A. Ministry to Israel 10:5-15
  B. Warning to people 10:16-23
  C. Instructions to Apostles 10:23-33
  D. Negative response to the gospel 10:34-39
  E. Promise to those who respond positively 10:40-42
	I. Witness concerning John 11:1-30
	  A. Response to John's question
	  B. Witness concerning question
	  C. Reproach on cities
	  D. Invitation to those who accept John
	II. Conflict with Pharisees
	  A. Accusations of Sabbath Breaking 12:1-45
	  B. Accusations of association
	  C. Seeking a sign
	III. Conflict with Jesus' Family 12:46-50
		I. Jesus' Use of Parables 13:1-9
		  A. Parable of the sower —
		  B. Why Jesus used parables — 13:10-17
		II. First Group of Kingdom Parables
		  A. Wheat and tares — 13:24-30
		  B. Growing seed — 13:31-32
		  C. Leaven — 13:33
		III. Parenthetical Statements
		  A. According to prophecy — 13:34-35
		  B. Explanation of tares parable — 13:36-43
		IV. Second Group of Kingdom Parables
		  A. Treasure — 13:44
		  B. Pearl — 13:45-46
		  C. Net — 13:47-50
		V. Summary Statement — 13:51-52

11. Marriage - Divorce - Remarriage: Narrative #5

Matthew 19 contains key information about Jesus' teaching concerning marriage and divorce. This study tries to correct certain misunderstandings about what Jesus is actually saying about who is guilty or innocent in these situations. (Matthew 19)

_____

_____

Intro - Jesus completes His ministry in Galilee and heads for Jerusalem

_____

_____

Road to Jerusalem – 19:1-20:34

Trip to Jerusalem – 19:1-2 _____

_____

Confrontation with Pharisees – 19:3-15 _____

_____

Vs. 3 _____

Deut. 24:1-4 _____

_____

Vs. 4-6 – Question concerning divorce _____

_____

Genesis 2:24 _____

Matthew 19:7-8 – Why did Moses "Command" divorce? _____

_____

Vs. 9 _____

_____

Only sexual sin was cause for divorce according to the Old Testament.

_____

_____

Debate:

- ADULTEROUS MARRIAGES _____

  _____

- ADULTRY = COVENANT BREAKING _____

  _____

Vs. 10 _____

_____

_____

Vs. 11 _____

_____

_____

Vs. 12 _____

_____

Summary

When it comes to offenses: _____

_____

_____

_____

Marriage comes from God _____
_____
_____

If marriage is dissolved _____
_____
_____

Comparative Passage

_____
_____
_____

Matthew 5:32 _____
_____
_____

In Matthew 19 Jesus talks about the _____ party, in Matthew 5 He talks about the _____ party.

Matthew 5:32 shows _____
_____
_____

    The offence _____
    The offence _____

Matthew 19 shows: _____
_____
_____
_____

Hypocrisy _____
_____
_____

The only cause _____
_____
_____
_____
_____

Luke 16:18 _____
_____
_____

Mark 10:1-12 _____
_____
_____
_____

I Corinthians 7

See Series: I Corinthians for Beginners - Lesson #4

_____
_____
_____
_____
_____
_____
_____

IV. NARRATIVE 13:53-17:27	IV. DISCOURSE 18:1-35	V. NARRATIVE 19:1-22:46
Jesus' Identity	Relationships	Ministry in Judea

I. Rejection at Nazareth - 13:53-14:12
II. Ministry to the Masses
  A. 5,000 fed - 14:13-21
  B. Healings by touching - 14:34-36
  C. Woman's daughter healed - 15:21-28
  D. Healings of sick and crippled - 15:29-31
  E. 4,000 fed - 15:32-39
  F. Healing of epileptic boy - 17:9-13
III. Response to Pharisees
  A. Breaking traditions - 15:1-20
  B. Ask for a sign - 16:1-12
IV. Ministry to Apostles
  A. By miracles performed
    1. Walking on water - 14:22-33
    2. Transfiguration - 17:1-8
    3. Coin in the fish - 17:9-17
  B. By teaching concerning
    1. True defilement - 15:15-20
    2. Teaching of the Pharisees - 16:1-12
    3. The church - 16:13-20
    4. The crucifixion - 16:21-28, 17:9-13, 17:22-33
	I. Basic Premise: Care for Each Soul 18:1-5
	  A. Character of people in Kingdom
	  B. Warning about offenses - 18:6-10
	    Parable about lost sheep - 18:11-14
	II. Dealing with Conflict:
	  Direct Confrontation - 18:15-20
	  A. Procedure - 18:15-17
	  B. Authority - 18:18-20
	III. Basis for Relationships:
	  Unconditional Forgiveness
	  A. The old standard - 18:21
	  B. Standard in the Kingdom - 18:22
	  C. Summary - 18:35
	    Parable - 18:23-34
		I. Road to Jerusalem
		  A. Descent to Jerusalem - 19:1-2
		  B. Confrontation with Pharisees - 19:3-12
		  C. Blessing of children - 19:13-15
		  D. Rich young man - 19:16-22
		  E. Teaching to the disciples
		    1. Riches - 19:23-30
		    2. Wages for laborers - 20:1-16
		    3. Prophecy of the cross - 20:17-19
		  F. Request from mother of James and John - 20:20-28
		  G. Pleading from the blind man - 20:29-34
		II. Jerusalem
		  A. Triumphal entry - 21:1-11
		  B. Jesus in the temple
		    1. Cleansing of temple - 21:12-22:46
		    2. Withered fig tree - 21:18-22
		    3. Confrontation
		      Elders and Priests - 21:22-14
		      Herodians - 22:15-22
		      Sadducees - 22:23-33
		      Pharisees - 22:34-36

V. DISCOURSE 23:1-25:46	VI. NARRATIVE 26:1-28:20
Rejection and Judgment	Death/Resurrection/Commission

I. NARRATIVE 1:1-4:23 Beginnings of the Gospel	I. DISCOURSE 5:1-7:29 Sermon on the Mount	II. NARRATIVE 8:1-9:34 Jesus' Power

I. Genealogy — 1:1-17
II. Birth — 1:18-25
III. Magi — 2:1-12
IV. Egypt — 2:13-15
V. Massacre & Return — 2:16-23
VI. John the Baptist — 3:1-17
VII. Temptations — 4:1-11
VIII. Galilee & Disciples — 4:12-25
	I. Beatitudes 5:1-16
	II. The Law 5:17-48
	III. Relationship with God 6:1-34
	IV. Relationship with others 7:1-12
	V. The way of life 7:13-29
		I. Miracles — 8:1-17
		  A. Leper Cleansed
		  B. Centurion's slave
		  C. Peter's mother-in-law
		II. Teaching - would be disciples 8:18-22
		III. Miracles — 8:23-9:8
		  A. Calming the storm
		  B. Cast out demons/Paralytic cured
		IV. Teaching — 9:9-17
		  A. Matthew called
		  B. Accusations
		  C. John's Disciples
		V. Miracles — 9:18-34
		  A. Official's daughter
		  B. Woman with hemorrhage
		  C. Dumb and demon possessed
		VI. Jesus, Lord of Harvest — 9:35-38

II. DISCOURSE 9:35-10:42 Discourse to the Twelve	III. NARRATIVE 11:1-12:50 Jesus and Skepticism	III. DISCOURSE 13:1-52 Parables of the Kingdom

I. Granting of the power 10:1
II. Name of the Apostles 10:2-4
III. Instructions concerning their Mission
  A. Ministry to Israel 10:5-15
  B. Warning to people 10:16-23
  C. Instructions to Apostles 10:23-33
  D. Negative response to the gospel 10:34-39
  E. Promise to those who respond positively 10:40-42
	I. Witness concerning John 11:1-30
	  A. Response to John's question
	  B. Witness concerning question
	  C. Reproach on cities
	  D. Invitation to those who accept John
	II. Conflict with Pharisees 12:1-45
	  A. Accusations of Sabbath Breaking
	  B. Accusations of association
	  C. Seeking a sign
	III. Conflict with Jesus' Family 12:46-50
		I. Jesus' Use of Parables 13:1-9
		  A. Parable of the sower —
		  B. Why Jesus used parables — 13:10-17
		II. First Group of Kingdom Parables
		  A. Wheat and tares — 13:24-30
		  B. Growing seed — 13:31-32
		  C. Leaven — 13:33
		III. Parenthetical Statements
		  A. According to prophecy — 13:34-35
		  B. Explanation of tares parable — 13:36-43
		IV. Second Group of Kingdom Parables
		  A. Treasure — 13:44
		  B. Pearl — 13:45-46
		  C. Net — 13:47-50
		V. Summary Statement — 13:51-52

12. Rejection and Judgement: Discourse #5

In this lesson Mike examines Jesus' response to those who rejected Him. A response that will pronounce a judgement on the religious leaders of that time as well as a long prophetic discourse about the destruction of Jerusalem and His return at the end of the world. (Matthew 23:1-25:46)

_____
_____

Intro - Jesus responds to those who reject Him.

_____
_____

Warning against Pharisees – Matthew 23:1-12

Vs. 1-4 _____
_____
_____

Vs. 5-7 _____
_____
_____

Vs. 8-10 _____
_____
_____

Vs. 11-12 _____
_____
_____

The Eight Woes – 23:13-36

Old Testament Prophets preaching style:

    A. _____
    B. _____
    C. _____
    D. _____

The eight woes:

5. _____
6. _____
7. _____
8. _____

1. _____
2. _____
3. _____
4. _____

Jesus' Lament Over Jerusalem – 13:37-39

_____
_____

Discourse on Judgment – Chapters 24-25

_____
_____

24:1-2 _____
_____

Two Questions:

1. When _____?
2. What _____?

Three Major Periods:

1. Panorama
2. Telescope – 70 AD
3. Telescope – END

Panorama – 24:4-14

Vs. 4 _____
_____

Vs. 5-8 _____
_____

Vs. 9-12 _____
_____

Vs. 13 _____

Vs. 14 _____

Telescope #1 – 70 AD – 24:15-35

_____

Vs. 15-18 _____

Vs. 19-21 _____

Vs. 22 _____

Vs. 23-26 _____

Vs. 27 _____

Vs. 28 _____

Vs. 29 _____

Vs. 30-31 _____

- Son of Man _____

- Angel/Messenger _____

Vs. 32-35 _____

_____

Telescope #2 – END – Matthew 24:36-44

_____

_____

Vs. 36 _____

Vs. 37-39 _____

Vs. 40-41 _____

Vs. 42-44 _____

_____

Exhortation to Vigilance – 24:45-25:30

A. Parable of evil slave – vs. 45-51 _____

_____

_____

B. Parable of 10 virgins – 25:1-13 _____

_____

_____

C. Parable of the Talents – 25:14-30 _____

_____

_____

Judgment Scene – 25:31-46

_____

_____

_____

13. From Passover to Communion: Narrative #6

In the final lesson of this series Mike will review the main events of Jesus' 'Passion' and focus in on the history of the Jewish Passover and its transition to the meal of remembrance that Christians around the world observe. (Matthew 26:1-28:20)

_____

_____

Review Outline – Narrative #6

Narrative _____

_____

Discourse _____

_____

Four Main Events:

A. _____

B. _____

C. _____

D. _____

History of the Passover – Ex. 12

_____

_____

Exodus 12:1-13 _____

_____

Exodus 12:23-28 _____

_____

Passover Meal

A. Table with Cushion _____

_____

_____

B. Food and Drinks _____
_____

C. Four Cups of Wine _____
_____

D. Order of Meal _____
_____
_____

   1. Lesson of the Towel – John 13:5-10 _____
   _____
   _____

   2. Revealing of the False Disciple – Matthew 26:20-25 _____
   _____
   _____

   3. Institution of the Lord's Supper _____
   _____
   _____

Jesus' Sacrifice:
- Pure Life   = _____
- Divine Nature   = _____

Matthew's Conclusion
_____
_____
_____

IV. NARRATIVE 13:53-17:27 — Jesus' Identity

I. Rejection at Nazareth - 13:53-14:12
II. Ministry to the Masses
   A. 5,000 fed - 14:13-21
   B. Healings by touching - 14:34-36
   C. Woman's daughter healed - 15:21-28
   D. Healings of sick and crippled - 15:29-31
   E. 4,000 fed - 15:32-39
   F. Healing of epileptic boy - 17:9-13
III. Response to Pharisees
   A. Breaking traditions - 15:1-20
   B. Ask for a sign - 16:1-12
IV. Ministry to Apostles
   A. By miracles performed
      1. Walking on water - 14:22-33
      2. Transfiguration - 17:1-8
      3. Coin in the fish - 17:9-17
   B. By teaching concerning
      1. True defilement - 15:15-20
      2. Teaching of the Pharisees - 16:1-12
      3. The church - 16:13-20
      4. The crucifixion - 16:21-28, 17:9-13, 17:22-33

V. DISCOURSE 23:1-25:46 — Rejection and Judgment

I. Warning Against Pharisees - 23:1-12
II. Seven Woes - 23:13-36
III. Lament over Jerusalem - 23:37-39
IV. Discourse on Judgment
   A. Panorama of History - 24:1-14
   B. Telescope of fall of Jerusalem - 24:15-35
   C. Telescope to Second Coming - 24:36-44
   D. Exhortations to vigilance
      1. Parable of Evil Slave - 24:45-51
      2. Parable of Virgins - 25:1-13
      3. Parable of Talents - 25:14-30
   E. Judgment Scene - 25:31-46

IV. DISCOURSE 18:1-35 — Relationships

I. Basic Premise: Care for Each Soul 18:1-5
   A. Character of people in Kingdom
   B. Warning about offenses - 18:6-10
   C. Parable about lost sheep - 18:11-14
II. Dealing with Conflict: Direct Confrontation - 18:15-20
   A. Procedure - 18:15-17
   B. Authority - 18:18-20
III. Basis for Relationships: Unconditional Forgiveness
   A. The old standard - 18:21
   B. Standard in the Kingdom - 18:22
   C. Summary - 18:35
      Parable - 18:23-34

V. NARRATIVE 19:1-22:46 — Ministry in Judea

I. Road to Jerusalem
   A. Descent to Jerusalem - 19:1-2
   B. Confrontation with Pharisees - 19:3-12
   C. Blessing of children - 19:13-15
   D. Rich young man - 19:16-22
   E. Teaching to the disciples
      1. Riches - 19:23-30
      2. Wages for laborers - 20:1-16
      3. Prophecy of the cross - 20:17-19
   F. Request from mother of James and John - 20:20-28
   G. Pleading from the blind man - 20:29-34
II. Jerusalem
   A. Triumphal entry - 21:1-11
   B. Jesus in the temple
      1. Cleansing of temple - 21:12-22:46
      2. Withered fig tree - 21:18-22
      3. Confrontation
         Elders and Priests - 21:22-14
         Herodians - 22:15-22
         Sadducees - 22:23-33
         Pharisees - 22:34-36

VI. NARRATIVE 26:1-28:20 — Death/Resurrection/Commission

I. The Final Hours with the Disciples
   A. Anointing and Betrayal - 26:1-16
   B. The Last Supper - 26:17-29
   C. Gethsemene - 26:30-56
II. Trial before Caiaphas - 26:57-75
   Trial before Pilate - 27:1-31
III. The crucifixion and burial - 27:33-56
IV. The Resurrection and Commission - 28:1-20

I. NARRATIVE 1:1-4:23	I. DISCOURSE 5:1-7:29	II. NARRATIVE 8:1-9:34
Beginnings of the Gospel	Sermon on the Mount	Jesus' Power

I. Genealogy — 1:1-17
II. Birth — 1:18-25
III. Magi — 2:1-12
IV. Egypt — 2:13-15
V. Massacre & Return — 2:16-23
VI. John the Baptist — 3:1-17
VII. Temptations — 4:1-11
VIII. Galilee & Disciples — 4:12-25
	I. Beatitudes 5:1-16
	II. The Law 5:17-48
	III. Relationship with God 6:1-34
	IV. Relationship with others 7:1-12
	V. The way of life 7:13-29
		I. Miracles — 8:1-17
		  A. Leper Cleansed
		  B. Centurion's slave
		  C. Peter's mother-in-law
		II. Teaching - would be disciples 8:18-22
		III. Miracles — 8:23-9:8
		  A. Calming the storm
		  B. Cast out demons/Paralytic cured
		IV. Teaching 9:9-17
		  A. Matthew called
		  B. Accusations
		  C. John's Disciples
		V. Miracles — 9:18-34
		  A. Official's daughter
		  B. Woman with hemorrhage
		  C. Dumb and demon possessed
		VI. Jesus, Lord of Harvest — 9:35-38

II. DISCOURSE 9:35-10:42	III. NARRATIVE 11:1-12:50	III. DISCOURSE 13:1-52
Discourse to the Twelve	Jesus and Skepticism	Parables of the Kingdom

I. Granting of the power 10:1
II. Name of the Apostles 10:2-4
III. Instructions concerning their Mission
  A. Ministry to Israel 10:5-15
  B. Warning to people 10:16-23
  C. Instructions to Apostles 10:23-33
  D. Negative response to the gospel 10:34-39
  E. Promise to those who respond positively 10:40-42
	I. Witness concerning John 11:1-30
	  A. Response to John's question
	  B. Witness concerning question
	  C. Reproach on cities
	  D. Invitation to those who accept John
	II. Conflict with Pharisees 12:1-45
	  A. Accusations of Sabbath Breaking
	  B. Accusations of association
	  C. Seeking a sign
	III. Conflict with Jesus' Family 12:46-50
		I. Jesus' Use of Parables 13:1-9
		  A. Parable of the sower —
		  B. Why Jesus used parables — 13:10-17
		II. First Group of Kingdom Parables
		  A. Wheat and tares — 13:24-30
		  B. Growing seed — 13:31-32
		  C. Leaven — 13:33
		III. Parenthetical Statements
		  A. According to prophecy — 13:34-35
		  B. Explanation of tares parable — 13:36-43
		IV. Second Group of Kingdom Parables
		  A. Treasure — 13:44
		  B. Pearl — 13:45-56
		  C. Net — 13:47-50
		V. Summary Statement — 13:51-52

BibleTalk.tv is an Internet Mission Work.

We provide textual Bible teaching material on our website and mobile apps for free. We enable churches and individuals all over the world to have access to high quality Bible materials for personal growth, group study or for teaching in their classes.

The goal of this mission work is to spread the gospel to the greatest number of people using the latest technology available. For the first time in history it is becoming possible to preach the gospel to the entire world at once. BibleTalk.tv is an effort to preach the gospel to all nations every day until Jesus returns.

The Choctaw Church of Christ in Oklahoma City is the sponsoring congregation for this work and provides the oversight for the BibleTalk ministry team. If you would like information on how you can support this ministry, please go to the link provided below.

bibletalk.tv/support

> BibleTalk.tv is one of the **most-prolific uploaders** on Amazon Prime Video with more videos than any major Hollywood studio except Paramount Pictures.

THE WALL STREET JOURNAL.

Made in the USA
Columbia, SC
07 March 2025